Picnic on the Fault Line
and other poems

by Julia E. Tanner

Crippled Beagle Publishing, Knoxville, Tennessee
dyer.cbpublishing@gmail.com

Cover artwork "Possibility" by Julie Tanner, 2018
Cover design by Jody Dyer

ISBN-13: 978-1-7321555-9-6

Printed in the United States of America.

To my mother, who encouraged me to pursue and nourish my love of the arts.

Poems

Early Morning Words 1

The Garden.. 3

Eyes.. 7

Shadows... 9

Fantasies.. 11

Druid Memories.. 13

Pain Service 17

Marked by living.. 19

Summertime... 21

Tennessee Sundae.. 25

Dauphin Rondo 29

After a long day with the cello........................... 33

My Father... 37

Christmas Returns 41

Nature of Love 45

The Reprieve 47

Lexicon... 49

Goodbye, My Friend 53

Bled By Katrina 55

Overripe Strawberries... 61

Telemetry Dream.. 65

Summer Journey.. 67

Missing Parts... 69

Hands 71

Wraiths... 75

That High Note 77

Musical Montage...79

The tight shoe...81

Old Wounds...83

Jon, Dillon, Wayne, and Jude..................................85

Mercy, Dreaming Across Arkansas.............................89

Desultories 93

Sweet thang...95

Stained Couture...99

Labyrinth 103

Dearest Jenny...105

Going South...107

Moments 111

Strings 113

Grace 115

Casting Call 117

Spring Haiku 119

Like A Wild Meadow...121

Saying Yes...123

In Transit 125

Propinquity..127

Loss and Love in the Circles of Life 129

To Anders, The New One 133

Nightmare...135

Downtown Haiku...137

Shadow Haiku 139

Longing for Lipstick..141

On The Bus 143

Eternity 145

Daisies 147

Museum 149

Chance Meet 151

Fly Free 153

Picnic on the Fault Line 155

Christmas Dreams 157

Afternoon Spent With My Mother's Poetry 161

Mirror 163

Truth 165

Old Style 167

Prayer in the Cloister 169

Evolving Limitations 171

Saint Mary Time 175

December Muse 177

Your Gentle 181

Because of the Moon 183

1989

Early Morning Words

Not yet eight
fog still reclines heavily on wet grass
birds have been chirping for hours
the refrigerator patiently hums on.

Already, waves of syllables have gushed
into my just aroused consciousness.
Awakened by radio news of hurricanes
the spread of AIDS in prison
governments on the slide, but at least
the Bush likes trees.

Words from my children
struggling to start their day
with the search for clean clothes
and library books on the loose
lunch money in neatly inscribed envelopes
bus notes, gym notes
and words on cereal boxes
reiterate fat content and vitamin counts.

The technicolor clarity of words brought
by an international phone line
from the opposite side of our spinning globe
with sweet familiar inflections
of a dear friend long gone
tickle my ear and soul leaving me incredulous
at the reality of the distance separating us.

The wet newspaper words rub off
on my fingers: murder for fun
high school hostage dramas, death
destruction and furniture ads bring me
reluctantly into the beginning of a new day.

In trying to decipher the mystery behind
the fibrous hull of an obscure Chinese squash

1

I consult a lengthy tome:
The Definitive Guide To Fruits and Vegetables
and learn much
about fourteen other varieties of squash.

The unpunishable crime of words overheard
is then compounded as the idea for this poem
springs to mind and begins to ferment
in this roiling vat of words between my ears.

Thankfully, I consider my oatmeal in silence
and anticipate the creation of wordless sound
made by bow caressing string.

—1989

The Garden

sleek furred hooves hesitantly
stepping from the blurred mist of the woods

into my little piece of earth
ever-changing with the season
now in the stormy throes of late summer

a riot of life underfoot, passing constancy
out on the road
the house vibrates in answer
seeking is

sublimation passes for passion
the energy reappears floating in the air
enters assorted crania
through unassuming ears

tilled with love and care
many heaping servings of the coming best
the happy compost of the mind
ripening with age into fertile soil

And now the decision to plant
inevitable, ever-changing
in output

the owner of the furry hooves
bends to munch my garden's yield

—1989

1990

Eyes

eyes, I mean eyes. why why
they could create an opening
and then you might invite another in
or they could send a person away
you could just end up wondering and wondering
can you really trust the enigmatic
language of eyes?

and words change the focus
you have seen it happen again, again
to so many whom you know and knew
and then there was last February
when the winds blew so coldly past the sun

but don't deny those
who every once in a little while
come shining through clear,
sincerely, wide open,
eyes.

—1990

Shadows

shadows cut across the periphery of my sight
the brightness of my centering is cast into doubt
a pair of eyes is caught in focus
but casts quickly away

the leaves of trees whisper to the wind
the pages torn are still the pages
which turn either way

air vibrates in lucid color with the passing sounds
the essence of one hundred individuals
briefly joined, and then gone
though truly unending

then the stars came out, and the wet moonlight
enveloped the vibrating air still fresh
with the flush of melody
and I was glad I had been there

now the new pale moon shadows cross boldly
and I kiss them, and invite them to enter my own
wet darkness but they have gone
and so I wait
knowing we will come again

—1990

Fantasies

thought, internally fleshed out
into possible realities
grows in living detail until it edges into our lives
moving us to do, to go, to believe
to become part of
the constantly unfolding
present

live your fantasies they said
crazed by their worship of the moment
the ensuing reality
more often did not live up to the imagination
other times, far exceeding dreamy projections

now as the decades unfold, I more often ask
what have I learned from this?
on the defensive, I boldly state,
yes! I, me, myself, I know they are fantasies only
I, I, I can indulge them, but they will not bend
my connection to the overflowing moment

but step outside this momentum of thought
to question and feel the slow relentless turning
of the wheel of fortune
unbidden, oblivious to mere will
despite the wishes of my yearning ego,
the turnings of my path proceed
far less self directed than I believe

but if we do not dream
surely we become mired
in the sticky morass of daily details
words from without envelop
every waking moment
and to surrender wholly to those of others
is a kind of living death

be brave and let your fantasies
bloom as you dream
admire them in their fullness
and then take one that you wish
to color, gently, the winding edges
of your always changing path

—1990

Druid Memories

The old carved limestone
worn down by wind and rain
further softened by furry moss.

New raindrops glistened on the zinnias
and the delicate touch of scent
brought inexplicable tears to my eyes.

Ancient pines and magnolias reigned
reaching far above any mere homes
and they spoke silently as I dared
to enter their realm.

I congratulated the roots
breaking the puny sidewalk
attempting to impose rectangular order
upon such magnificence.

The pale gray of the tiny gravestone,
inscribed, 1817, at the age of ten months
and the name was gone.

I knew that babe must have lain
contentedly suckling
beneath the cool boughs of my new friend.

And I wanted to lie down
in the wet grass under the leaves,
and let the force of life of this being
penetrate me.

—1990

13

1992

Pain Service

Pain served in heaping shiny portions
by the surgical team's
skillful slicing and stitching

Immediate relief is promised
by the little flick of a button
clipped to your regulation gown

All guaranteed and serviced
by the cheerful blue coated ranks
of the Pain Service

Quick, efficient, gone
narcotics direct to the spinal cord
but then my body is happy
and I am gone, too

—1992

17

Marked by living

of the many remarkable abilities of our bodies,
savor especially the ready absorption
by our most visible outer casing
of each passing moment into display,
from subtle to glaring, upon ourselves

a small bruise upon my inner arm
reminds of a distracted clumsy moment
rushing too close by solid furniture

faint marks on a tender portion of neck
tell tales of impassioned kisses
stolen in brief retreat from daily cares

the fingertips, worn and calloused
about closely clipped nails,
leave faint streams of music vibrating
in the air through which they pass

an invisible soreness in the thighs
leaves lips turning toward a smile
from happy moments of exertion

the map of lines about the eyes
and forehead and mouth combine with
silver strands of hair to tell long stories
of years spent engaged in life

scraped elbows bring another rueful
and smiling turning of the lips
while a long scar can mist my eyes with joy
at the knowledge of two beautiful children

a faintly darkened area on the inner curve
of my left breast once again entwines
these memories, distant and present
with the sweet sound of cello
pressed closely to my body

so I counsel myself to not fear
inevitable new marks however long
or painful, to soon be left by surgeons
in the name of improvement

but to welcome them into the ongoing history
already recorded upon myself

—1992

Summertime

Sweet hint of pink mimosa blooms
peeking through my tall maple,
hued in its deep gold green,
rich with the height of summer.

The marigolds shiver in the breeze,
the orange of day lilies
is a memory only,
remembered by their dead proud shafts.

Trees wave their foliage proudly,
the field is rising up toward the sun,
and all of it feeds my soul
and sparks the underside of my vitality.

An evening so sweet.
The heat has slid away on the breeze
and I float on the soft layers of summer.

—1992

1993

Tennessee Sundae

free on my fence row
alongside these plump blackberries
the delight of Queen Ann's lacy head
and the black-eyed beauty, Susan

other blossoms all pink and fuzzy
pixie's slippers stand by the poisonous poke
blooming elderberry inviting
to come back later

biggest dark and juicy fruits
are farthest back in the shade
beckoning you to dare reach
through thorns and brambles

purple fingers with scratches
small price for the sweet reminders
of early morning communion
graced by gently buzzing bees

berries dropped to the ground
are no cause for consternation
seeding promises of future fruits

the dark mound in my bucket
grows as I delve further
into the singing summer brush

a hawk flies through
the brown blur of rabbit's dash

aligned with the earth now
in pursuit of the taste of summer

I return to my home

—1993

1994

Dauphin Rondo

An unrestrained chorus of many birds
a melodious herald of flocks
fleeing the heat of tropical lands
rejoicing calls weave into
the sinuous sound of the wind
caressing the tall swaying trees

 A short punctuation as a
a flatly curved magnolia leaf
drops to the waiting forest floor
adding itself to the carpet

Night falls
chattering birds quiet
the roaring wind in the trees
obscures the sounds
of humanity

Warm and snug in a little tent
raindrops add to the song of the night
a gentle syncopation
interrupted by soft sighs of pleasure
joined in the dark beneath
the wide canopy of live oak

Gentle grays of dawn
slip in to bring us forth
but it is the sweet calls
of the birds above us
which announce the new day.

—1994

1995

After a long day with the cello

so few notes
but played in so many ways
vibrating through my core
phrases contiguous
synched up
that special feel

music creates light
inside of us as
demands of its circuit
wear and drain at our centers

arms, fingers, souls
poured out to the senses
of the listeners
in attendance just then or later

we are yours
whoever (hearing) you may be
drink my vibrations
it pleases me
let them change you
for at least a moment

—1995

2002

My Father

I loved my Daddy.
He always had time for me
and my childish questions.
He died before I came of age:
I remember him saying that he would
Gladly give his life for mine
He meant it
But sacrifice:
Even for the daughter of a preacher
Not a comfortable gift to think of accepting.

Now my daughters are of the same age
As I was when he died.
I would give up my life
So that they might continue theirs
But I only tell them that I love them
Give of life to them
In all those ways that I can find.

He was only ten years older than I am now
When his heart stopped.
His gift of life and love and faith still live in me.
The leap of faith which brought me back
Home to the church:
As real as his Bible on my bookshelf.
I feel his smile from heaven.

An old child now, I hold to my heart
The gift of the Father's sacrifice.
The holy only child given to us:
The many children
Living in a fog of ignorance
Made uncomfortable by the truth
I pray that my life will be a gift also.

—2002

2003

Christmas Returns

An angry young woman in her patched jeans
self-absorbed, proud
filled with the arrogance of youth.
In mid-December
striding the streets of New York City
shop windows filled with twinkling lights
shouting, Big Sale! Buy Here! Spend!

She eyes the wet trees for sale on the sidewalk
and the passed-out man
clinging to one in his drunken dream state.
The trees look like decapitated heads to her:
cut from their life-giving roots,
now destined to shrivel and die
over the next few weeks.
A symbol for a ritual that she has decided
will no longer touch her.
But some still soft part of her mourns
for the murdered trees.

Fifteen Decembers later
and that still soft part has grown.
Maybe after the birth
of two beautiful daughters.
Maybe at the relief for her hardened soul
in the warm summer evenings
of honeysuckle scented Tennessee.

The little red house with the tin roof:
her clothesline was strung
between two big oaks in the backyard.
Another big tree shades the rickety front porch
with the rocking chair.

She doesn't know why tears come to her eyes
when she hears The Lord's Prayer.

Stronger than a tornado's wind,
it was the force of the Spirit that drew her back
to the Church of her youth she knows now.
Jesus had never stopped waiting for her,
and He was waiting
for all of his children to come home
to join in the celebration of his birth.

All the little ones were singing
Away in A Manger.
They were carrying handmade decorations
for the big tree in the sanctuary
a symbol of life, growth, and joy.
Grown for that purpose
later it would provide warmth
in a wood burning stove
for more of God's children.

One snowy evening in December,
she saw the joy in her own daughters' eyes
as they stepped between the rows
of so many little Christmas trees, to pick one.
It would find a home with them
filling the room with its earthy sweet aroma
and under the branches, gifts to one another.
Now a symbol of the greatest gift of God to us:
His Son.

Separated by her own choice from God
in her youth, her own roots had felt severed.
The source of salvation was always there.
The path: the human heart
open to the love of the Christ child.

—2003

2004

Nature of Love

The warmth of a smile
reflected in the eyes,
then seen as a promise
of a soul: open

Perhaps then misunderstood
across the divide of air, shared
in our mutual breathing
followed by complications
preemptive anticipations

Further then exacerbated by
long histories of sad meetings
hopes dashed in turbulent reality
time spent and gone.
no return

Too many misunderstood words
even more left unspoken
Be quiet and listen
perhaps you will hear, and feel

A call to love humanity in all its myriad
wrinkled, slick, silent, noisy, angry, sweet,
tired, bored, smelly, fragrant, foul, abrasive,
handsome, delicious, intriguing, confounding,
appealing, and mysterious forms

Love with no thought of return
could it really be possible?
We are promised that it is the true way
To give such love is a freedom
a liberation of the soul's potential,
to openly receive is more difficult.

—2004

The Reprieve

The reprieve was for twenty years
but I didn't know that
as it was so granted by God.
It felt like it could have been the rest of my life
(a longer one that is)
but for the little I knew
that could have been days or less.

So I asked myself
What fruit has been born of this gift?
This gift of living time?

In this time, two beautiful children
helped and taught and loved through youth
adolescent pains and struggles
now arriving into their young adultness
discovering independently their own
potentials to love, to create, to share joy
with friends and lovers they have found.

In this time, many hours spent teaching others
to express outwardly their inner music
to find deeper spiritual places
to more fully show love to others.
Surely this time was as much a gift
to this giver
as it was to the receivers.

In this time, so much music made by me
and my old cello and my old bow.
I love that my tones may be heard reverberating
on many discs, tapes, records, TV's and radios
those vibrations out there, disembodied
but maybe making the world a little lighter.

In this time, countless performances
I treasure having brought a smile, a tear, a sigh
to another soul
with a phrase well turned, or a note
containing more than a note's full of vibrations.
My hope:
that the butterfly effect goes double for music.

In this time, communicating beyond music:
speaking, loving, being loved, listening,
touching, writing, laughing, and being there.
I wish I could say that I used well
all twenty years' worth.

In this time, more hoping
that this time I got the math wrong again
and my reprieve continues.
Another good knock upside this hard head
from our all-knowing and loving God.
I thank you and I praise you.

In this time, my list of worthy fruits all,
gifts to others in my human family
those given with love, care, and compassion.

And a list of produce from time squandered?
Worthwhile to be learned from:
Teachers of humility.

—2004

Lexicon

A lexicon of life and love and alliteration
All about and around human abstraction
Being bitter and buttered, bound by
Creation, crafty concepts, carefully
Destroying deifying disturbing doubts
Eagerly enjoying energy empathetically
Forever free fascinating friends
Going gaga, getting grateful gasps
Having hungry happenings however
I inspire impetuous insinuations
Just jockeying for jests
Knowing Krispy Kreme kan
Link longings, laughter, legato lines
Making much of monstrous
    mellow mastications
Not nonsense now
Only openness, offspring of
Patient parents, pouting pundits probably
Quite quiescently: quiet quandary
Rasping really rare rhythmic rhymes
So some see sounds silly, sassy, sick
Though talking through timeless tiny
    tintinnabulation's
Unable unceasingly unable unwind
Very variable vanity, vainly
    vindicates vagueness
Whatever wanted, winsomely
    wantonly writhe, wobbledy weave
Xeric IneXorably, eXpressively XL X-ray
Yet youth, yearning, yawning, yeah
Zig zag zygote, zesty zoo.

—2004

2005

Goodbye, My Friend

The phone call came late at night
I was on the opposite coast
An old friend had died at the age of sixty-three
His body was still in Mexico

Really, he was more than a friend
The love of my life when in my wild 20's
Him in his 30's

Always full of love and swagger
A man with no fear
Endlessly fascinated by the world
But especially by its inhabitants

His was the uncanny ability to be in the moment
More fully than you had ever thought possible
Pretense angered him,
But he could tell a story forever
His smile would melt you
Topped as it was by those pale blue eyes

Then the time came
And your days together were over
People change, I wanted a family
He said he would never have children
And then he would tell that story (again)
His drunken father screaming at his mother
Throwing the Christmas tree
Through the front window

He visited me. I visited him.
The phone conversations became less frequent
His marriage decades later bore fruit
(He denied wanting) two beautiful daughters

When I met them
The younger kept calling me mommy
The older one showed me her book

His last few years had started a downward slide
He left his family. He had a heart attack.
He would not return my calls.
Friends said he was depressed and drifting
Then that last conversation
It seemed he had lost his will
To live, to laugh, to love, why?
Always a devout atheist
Raised in a Catholic family
Constantly running in the opposite direction

Age comes upon us
We see an endgame approaching
The meaninglessness of life so eloquently
Espoused by those who deny the existence of God
Must look increasingly hurtful, illogical
Pain and depression constant companions

So now I regret that I didn't try a little harder
To be there for him
Even as he turned me away
I wish I could have found the words to turn his heart
Toward the warmth of God's love
God's peace and grace
Always there for any who want it
The incomparable assurance
Free with your faith.

—2005

Bled By Katrina

Sometimes the TV makes me cry.
Beloved steamy N'Awlins
home to my first season of adulthood
battered by a ferocious storm
gutted by overflowing levees
the sorrow magnified
by human inadequacy.

Images of those narrow streets:
bare arms outstretched
from wrought iron balconies
fern fronds waving in the damp wind
bring a sweet breeze of memory.

We were hand in hand
atop one of those levees
on a crisp fall day overlooking
the mighty muddy Mississippi
He said, "Did you know
that most of the city
lies lower than the river?
That without these to hold it back,
there would be a great flood?"

It seemed an impossibility
but my thoughts were not there,
but with the reality of his warm hand in mine
a developing trust from the gentleness
of his kiss that seemed a promise
for the future, though that trust
long gone before the year had past.

I did not return to him
or the newly beloved city later that year.

But many stayed and more arrived
in that magical messy place
alive with the sound of music and celebration.

The city blooms year-round even with
the persistent undercurrent of desperate
poverty and its legion companions.
All those dreams shored up in those lives
trusting in those slopes of grass-covered earth
silently ringing their neighborhoods.
Dreams shored up
by their own sunny afternoons
now drowned in swirling toxic muck.

My TV cried out their misery of broken trust
dreams drowned: first the earth gave way
fellow sufferers turned on them
their rescuers passed them by
as they stood crying and waving
then more of humanity
(spared this time from mud and flood and loss)
chose not to come.
As they waited, dying in heat and brown waters,
the magical musical city
turned into the city of sorrow.

My story from years past felt inconsequential
though it wasn't for young me
and my tender heart then.
I had trusted him to love me
to look out for me.
But the promises had not been real
only imagined and hoped for
I thought I wanted to die at the betrayal
but instead I learned to trust less
at the drowning of my youthful dreams.

And in the week of Katrina so many cried out
How can they just leave us here?
Where is the help we were promised?
We didn't all just decide to stay.
Some had, some tried to leave,
but so many had no way to flee.
But they had trusted that the promise
of help from others was real.
Truly in need, surely they would receive it.
That all our lives would be valued equally.
We protested, we don't deserve this!
We trusted. We learned.

                                                    —2005

2006

Overripe Strawberries

June 1970 and my father dead:
a heart attack and gone that evening.
I answered my Mom's front door
expecting another casserole,
instead the funeral home messenger
handed me a paper bag.

Dad's glasses and neatly folded pajamas.
Cremation had been his choice.
I shouldn't have opened the bag:
I pictured flames. Those last
physical remnants unleashed the sad hurt
coalesced into tears and tears of pain and loss.

So Mom and I lived together that summer
at the family's summer house.
We had been six there, all together
in laughter, in tension, and that dance
that families do.   Then, I had sat on the porch
watching the world go by, reading
one book after another
basking in the glorious gift of summertime.

Now we were just two,
And this summer so different:
my Mommy struck down by grief,
but trying to put on her old face,
trying to stick to the routine.

Daddy's presence walked through
the kitchen and the garden
wafted out of an unopened book,
and left us stunned and leaden
in his absence.

Me, in my first year of adultness
But not yet quite knowing how to do that,
living again with my Mom for one last time,
but not knowing that, either.

(I write this at 56, and she is 93
and from here I know I should have savored
that last summer
of mother-daughter closeness.)

But no, I was my father's daughter
so eager to be independent while actually
freshly divorced, and numb from loss.
I had to find someone else to lean on:
a young man who would let me take his arm,
while working hard at my playing and forgetting.

The grief of youth becomes
energy eager to be spent
scrubbing floors, hauling heavy things,
running through wet grass, and not stopping.

I agreed to be the helper
of an ailing friend of the family.
I bathed her aging body, and washed her dishes
with only a sponge and a bar of Ivory soap:
precisely as she instructed me.

A blur of practice rooms and concerts
masked the dull ache in my head and soul.
Tchaikovsky resounded from wooden balconies,
and I played in the music competition
at the summer's end.
I came in second, again.

(Now I see second as a respectable accomplishment,
but back then, it just meant that you had lost.)

My mother was disappointed along with me.
I knew she wanted me to win.

Later in the day she went to the farmers market
and brought back some mushy strawberries.

I said, these don't look very good.
She said, that was all they had, and
I do know how you love strawberries.
I saw the love in her wanting to give them to me.
And I grew a little wiser that day when
I thankfully ate the overripe strawberries.

—2006

Telemetry Dream

The key was stuck in the lock
Though many were, and fewer weren't

Some are, though more aren't
How many, and how many times?
We can't know.

Questions flowing
Still no answers showing
Keep trudging, keep asking, and open up.

You set the lock.
Now try to remember why.
Doesn't matter if you remember how
Even if you do remember when
To ask for help, since it is all around you.

A quickly receding dream
Like the key
Reflecting in a bright pair of eyes:
Light filtering through your shadows.
The door opens, locked.
Be the flower as your petals extend.
Hear, feel, know the limitless warmth.

—2006

Summer Journey

Long slow Union Pacific train
Sliding through the soybean fields
Aching across hot land as far
As a human eye might see

Silver blue sky, double wide
Shimmered by tiny cloudlets
Lining up across the horizon

Breathless Tori sings,
"Let's go!"
in my air-conditioned pod of a car

Power poles stand at attention
Receding through mirages
Half transparent, demanding

It feels like a ragged map of my life.
I smile.

—2006

Missing Parts

His big eyes, rimmed with tears
As I touched his shoulder
Kissing the top of his balding head
He knew me
He was glad I was there
As he tried to speak
Each sentence ended before or after the verb
Frustration clouded former gladness in his eyes

Tubes and catheters led
To many glowing and beeping machines
Gathered tightly around the bed.
I prayed for God's healing presence.

The human circle moved loosely
About this inner circle
Of which he was the unwilling center

My heart hurt through thankfulness
For anything I could give
Knowing my helplessness at the witness
To our inevitable human reality
Bodies with finite endings
A progression, a mystery
Revealed in pain and ignorance
I encircled his failing body with mine

—2006

Hands

He said he knew it was me
When he saw my hand, ungloved

One among many standing in
A sea of coated backs and hatted heads

An unplanned encounter,
All the sweeter for that.
And a new-found intimacy
Amongst the whorls and digits
Of humanity's connections

—2006

2007

Wraiths

I know he's dead
But I saw him again

Striding across the street
Wearing the old green parka
That determined stare
On the chiseled Irish features
Overly confident swagger suffusing his moves

Just how he looked thirty years ago

And the city was wrong, too
Of course I knew it wasn't him
But the enigmatic half smile made my heart lurch

There are others, too
My sweet Dad, who's been gone much longer
Once he stood quietly amongst the trees
Behind the cemetery, as I laid flowers on his grave
More often, he's at church on Sunday morning
Singing in the choir, or sitting
Several rows behind the pew where I am sitting
Just out of sight, a warm presence
Making me smile

And another is one who is only heard:
My old friend, the quirky mathematician violinist
He whistled all his melodies backstage
After playing the concert
And now a presence is sounded there on some nights
A distantly trailing whistled first violin part
Years past his departing this plane.

But, my big brother
Why does he only come to me in dreams?
And why are all the ghosts men?
I don't believe in ghosts.

A lesson in our true nature
Our shared humanity?

—2007

That High Note

Undulating arpeggios herald arrival of The Season
A tickle of memories of that familiar song
Each year, the Christmas Concert
That high school gym hot on a cold winter night
A young soprano moves from triumphant audition
To the scary reality of the evening's performance
O Holy Night
The collective held breath at that high note
Will it be accolades and applause
Or a collective wince at that high note
Just a little cracked and sharp this year
Followed by kind and hollow words of praise?

Cut to now...
I am still in the orchestra, an arpeggio player
The melody is as beautiful as it always was
The words and harmony now resonate
With decades of my own Christmases

This year it's a young tenor given the guest spot
Now, thousands are out there in the audience
Many pitches elude him, but he doesn't seem to care
And the crowd goes wild
They love him and his sincerity and his going for it
They don't care about that high note

I glance around me to see the half-concealed winces
The raised eyebrows and rolled eyes
Among the players
But this time I am smiling with the audience

—2007

Musical Montage

Ever stop to wonder
so many photos and sketches of you
images left here and there
down through the years

Some you were in the background
other times you were part of a group playing
hundreds of weddings, actually
and more recitals, concerts, and rehearsals

Or maybe that rock festival
you were not in any of the bands
it was very hot, and you were young
so don't feel bad
that you were not entirely clothed

So many times, someone said,
can I take your picture?
and then more times they didn't
but others did, anyway
or you didn't know

All the ones in someone else's albums
that you never saw
you: the unnamed sleeping one or
smiling from the sidelines or
holding a cat, maybe your mouth was full
you had a goofy look on your face
your underwear was showing, you looked fat
you looked your age, you looked radiant
Your smile lit up the room

The bulbs were flashing that night
you were on stage at the little folk music club
valiantly playing the tambourine
and playing the cello
in a shell encrusted snakeskin skirt

The 1964 All State High School Orchestra or
three sisters playing trios on a warm summer day
or just a shot of someone else, you beside them
group shots: the lone cello player in a concert band
the symphony playing for the horse show
in Shelbyville TN, or the opening of a shopping mall
or a football stadium

So many personal and family photo opps
proud Mom with daughters or parents or friends
alongside a Yucatan cenote with a monkey
in the background, you climbing dripping
from the water, you smiling
from the zocalo cafe in Oaxaca

Flashback to Easter Sunday on 5th Ave.
New York City as you played Bach on the sidewalk
and lots of tourists took your picture that day
and all summer long in Central Park as long lines
queued up for free tickets to Shakespeare
and your hat was full

My sister sent me a very old photo
she had found at a yard sale
a family group of musicians posed
with their instruments though surely long dead
these many years later she loved the image
has it framed in her music room
it leaves her with a feeling of familiarity
risen from the past, now to be part of her present
nameless, abiding still together

A beloved family tintype sits on my mantel
two gentlemen posing
from more than one hundred years ago
Perhaps great uncles or distant cousins
but their names and stories are lost now
though their faces are part of my days
as they still gaze out, sitting together

—2007

The tight shoe

The shoe was on the right foot
But it was a pathetic sort of a day
Self-pity creeping around the edges of
Tired and overworked
But still a brain in overdrive
Running over actions and inactions:
Instant replays of my past

I was the one who didn't want the alimony
I returned everything
Happy just to leave with my freedom
My friends thought I was crazy
"He should have had to pay," they said.
There was real money to be had!

Later, again, I paid the bills
I held the home together
And I just got lies
And somebody else's debts
But once again, I just wanted my life back.
"You should have gotten a good lawyer,"
My friends said.

Such a sorry set of tales:
Admitting to myself that recently,
Taken once again.
Still paying, because
I wanted to do even more
Than just the right thing.
This time, my friends just shook their heads.

In the midst of this sorry litany,
I said a prayer:
Dear God, please forgive my unforgivingness

To those who have found me so easy to take,
To those I loved and who left me with only tears,
Help me to understand.
Help me to go forward.
Help me to forgive.

And then, came the image of turning my other cheek.
How much better to not have been the one who lied,
To not have been the one who took all he could get.
I knew it was good to not have been
The one who made all the mess and then just left,
Who justified exploitation and betrayal.

Now I willingly put the other shoe on.
They don't feel so tight:
Regrets receding into the light.

—2007

Old Wounds

Tears came to her eyes
And she started to choke up
Telling me a true story
A daughter wounded
By her mother's hurtful words
Except it was forty years ago
And still hurting like it was today
The wound open and raw
And the resentment fueling her actions

It was worse because the words
Came from one who loved her
Had nurtured her
And should have known better
Perhaps uttered without ill intent
Thoughtlessly on a day
When this Mom was hurting,
The old wounds from her own mother
Scratched open

I thought of what I had learned much later
How she felt weak resentful lowly
In her world daily laden
With dreams evaporated
Old age looming like a dark cloud ahead

And what salve could start the healing?
Apology, forgiveness, regret, more words
Or too late for the one carrying
All the memory and pain
And that one seeing no reason to forgive

Later she said she was thankful
To have never had a daughter
Fearful of passing it on
Punishing scars never to fade

We learn to remember that our tongues'
Utterances are powerful weapons
To think before speaking
To consider outcomes

Words loosed
Regardless of intent
Whether in honesty or
Impulsively blurted out
Results can reverberate
Through generations of tender hearts

—2007

Jon, Dillon, Wayne, and Jude

Dolly's on the wall, Ralph Stanley, too:
it's writers in the round
tourists do abound, and the hats are out
because it's a Nashville tradition
three chords and the truth

Jon's Mom wanted us to know
his nimble guitar pickin'
was entirely self-taught
the hit of his shows

Dillon's hair was wild and free
blissfully hatless
with a sheepish grin,
he cranked his volume up past three

Wayne reveled in his daring,
all boots and jeans and hat
a first timer in this ritual
of melodies and verse
his whole family there to hoot and holler

Jude's jeans were carefully torn
her makeup was perfect,
cleavage artfully arranged,
they rested gracefully on her old guitar

All about love and heartache
around we go
"Ah'd giv anythin' to hev you beck"

Each arrived with guitar in hand, but
only one's was graffiti laden:
markers, stickers, Dad's homegrown wisdom
and a telling moment, when he turned it over
to set a beer upon it, and it was his table, too

Struggling to get the G string in tune,
another remarked, I could use a tuner, but
that's kind of like a man asking for directions

—2007

2008

Mercy, Dreaming Across Arkansas

One singing harmony with herself
conciliatory tire treads humming
your cold, cold heart
kudzu obscured

It's just a song, but
why me, she thought, warming
why drive this delivery of love
through fields of rusty sorghum
edged with sumac
framed by regal ironweed?

Cornfields widening
curvy soft, furred green,
black accents: birds in distant formation

The driver of the big yellow school bus had said,
"You're no school girl!"

Pungent scent of skunk wakes me from this reverie
one oblivious egret winging high overhead
and below, silent sentinel silos saying nothing

A crushed armadillo
prehistoric remains return the mental road trip
to a straight painted line
for me to follow

And a surety settles inside
the whisper of the small still voice
this is your road

—2008

2009

Desultories

The library, the kitchen
A dusty floor on a sunny day, an unmade bed
A smiling bride bringing unbidden memories
Of misery and betrayal

An old story: my mother on a train, falling in love
A faded photo of her struggling daughter
A half-remembered melody
Lists of times and dates

The need for an oil change, a haircut
Another friend gone
A child's sad question
Another's bright smile

Thirsty plants, and hungry pets
Random, lengthy, palpable needs
A heart full of desire to give
Go, be, do, love, live

—2009

Sweet thang

Sum total of a fleeting relationship
I enter to pay at the market
And am greeted as "sweet thang" by the sweet thing
of a 19-year-old clerk with carefully coifed blonde hair.
As our brief transaction is completed,
I am addressed at least four more times as "sweet thang"
Should I return the compliment?
Me, the tired 59-year-old with the gray coming in good...
Say, I had said, not just "Thanks," but
"Why thank you so much, you sweet young thing!"
Most likely would have been viewed as ironic
No, more likely insulting, or perverted.
Or just accepted with a smile?
Wonder if it was her first day on the job.

—2009

2010

Stained Couture

A collection of old dresses and underwear
At the local museum

One elegant dress on display
A faded stain spreading over the belly

Slashes of brilliant red lipstick
On unsmiling lips
Echoing in the satin bows
Perched on ready hips

An exhibit of once exquisite gowns
Now on faceless mannequins
A small video screen shows the underpinnings
To these not quite human shapes

A corset creates a tiny waist
Small pads expand the hips
The brassiere creates petulantly pointing breasts
And bizarrely shaped shoes
Complete the pain of beauty

The Black Swan: a ball gown hand sewn
(by women, for women)
 of satin and silk velvet
My friend wonders,
Could they actually sit down in these dresses?

Long gloves and ornate perfume bottles
Further document the lives of the wealthy
Images admired by so many little girls
Poring over the glossy pages of fashion magazines
Looking in the mirror, examining waistlines
And breasts and feet, and finding them wanting

Yet some signs of humanity
Show in the display cases:
A scuffed heel, and that stain
On the white crepe dress
A faded collar and an uneven hemline
Tell of other stories unspoken here.

One more display reveals
The lives of the seamstresses
And runway models.
Low wages and tenement homes
Seated at long tables
Women in homespun wearing hairnets
Stitching and cutting the fantasies.

—2010

2013

Labyrinth

Palm Sunday in Nashville Tennessee
Lush rainy cool day
Early spring colored trees and flowers
Wet willow branches touched with vivid green
Tiny buds, leaves in waiting

A labyrinth is not a maze
And it was inside, in the church's basement
Larger than the ground floor of my home
Printed on white cloth
The color of lilacs just bloomed

After a fruitless search of the wet grounds
I heard the voices of my friends drifting up the stairs
From the silent and empty sanctuary
From below, telling stories of their sweet mother
The inimitable Gayle Alexander
Now on the other side of this veil of tears
Gifting us again, but with a labyrinth
Because she knew we needed one

It is a walk through the metaphors of life
Take off your shoes and find the entrance
Twists and turns will force your eyes on the ground
To focus only on your feet to stay true to the path
You traverse back at a sharp turn to see
Where you have just been
Covering the same ground again, almost

Then a long graceful curve swings you round
The perimeter: look up
See the whole expanse and beyond
To the faces of others you had forgotten
There with you on your journey
An inner smile embraces you as you reach the center
To see and smell the flame from a candle burning
Waiting just for you

Slide your bare feet into each indenture
Of the inner circle
To find the one for you
Close your eyes and breathe thanks
The many who have not yet entered
Continue to murmur

As you venture back out of the center to retrace
The curves and sharp turns with joy and regret
Knowing that soon you will leave the circle
Awkward angles feel gentler, the long smooth sweep
Along the outer edge feels even sweeter
The light from the center is yours to take with you
Out into the world
So you step out and find your shoes
Mindful of that other daily labyrinth
Awaiting your every step

Later, driving home,
A wild turkey runs out into the middle of road
And other cars are slowing too
People smiling, making room for her to live
On our paths

—2013

Dearest Jenny

So many more conversations we will never have
So many more times I wanted to walk with you
To sit with you, to smile with you
A path from tippy toed toddler
To compassionate young woman
Is treasure in my heart
A gift from your almost 27 years here with us
Still stunned, still shocked and sorrowing
That you are no longer with us in all these ways
But your spirit now burns warmly in all of us
Who were touched by your life
That loving brightness of your soul
Is multiplying out
Into this world
So much good sowed in so many lives
Radiates into our broken world
And that will never die

—Aunt Julie, 2013

Going South

Living in the city
embracing a dream
I could no longer remember
as it dissolved around me

whether to start again
to pursue another
replace the subway tunnel
with a clothes line in the back yard

goodbye friends and colleagues
hello new family not yet met
saying yes made simple
by the sweet smell of honeysuckle

—2013

2014

Moments

(With apologies to Frederick Buechner, who is quoted,
or rather paraphrased in the last two lines.)

Some memories still so clear
From so long ago

A clearing in the woods
A favorite spot for me as a child
As I returned home

In that remembered moment
A little bird dying on the ground
And my profound sadness
And a new knowledge of helplessness
In the face of death

A friend of a friend seeing me
with an open-faced sandwich
I think it was peanut butter and strawberry jam
Stepping quickly up and folding it closed,
And my irritation

Other moments: a sister asks,
Don't you remember??
She remembers clear as a bell
And I encounter a blank page

Others you had not thought of in so long
And then a smell, a song, or another's tale
Illumines that page that had been so dark

And then ones that one might wish had gone dark
And were no longer part of who we are
Choking tears while crouched
On the floor of a dark closet
News of death, and terrors of a tormentor's return.

Yes, life, full with the beautiful and terrible.
Do not be afraid.

—2014

Strings

A family of instruments
All with bows and four strings
Emerging from dusty cases

Requiring true patience and tolerance
Early efforts all scrapes and shrieks
Tuning struggles, recalcitrant pegs
Frustration at attempts
to glide horse hair on steel

In time, hands learn
Their place as a connector
To the heart

The reluctant left hand centers
Into the pulsing of the pitch
Tiny contact point of bow on string
Draws forth music from the player's soul
And the listeners become one in beauty

—2014

Grace

A gift found unwrapped
Most often in a place, unexpected
You felt you didn't deserve it
But the bright smile
The warm touch on your arm
Were yours to keep

Gentle coolness on the breeze
Of a hot day, you thought
You had set out to do the giving
And found yourself receiving
More than your imagination

Learning to trust again
Despite the ragged and hurting edges
Leap, anyway
To find a soft featherbed beneath you

Extend a hand to another's
Your soul delights in connection:
Cumulative resonance
And the lamps are lit

Soft thunder in the distance
A sweetening of the night air:
Fulfilled promise with the warm
And cleansing rain

Share the pain
In love we find the way beyond it
We unite as His body
And the grace is free

—2014

Casting Call

She yawned again
Considering casting all her day's plans
To the wind, in the trash

Another day and the mask feels tight
Member of a cast that she does not recall
Having ever chosen to audition for,
Nor having read the script

She thinks of her last name,
Same as one of the untouchable castes
In a faraway land that she has only
Walked in her dreams

Wondering, wandering, if this is the day
To truly cast off the old, the heavy,
The ill-fitting trappings of her life

—2014

Spring Haiku

mockingbird singing
violets shiver in the wind
clouds slide aside for blue

—2014

Like A Wild Meadow

my life revolves through its seasons,
a cool spring, a tangled profusion of tiny flowers
bring hope and promise on a cloudy day

the summer of lush green and thorny vines
heat of passion, running through these weeds:
falling to the ground, a satisfied exhaustion

as fall calms my meadow, I stop to look:
eyes caught by colorful leaves blown in
by a soft breeze, the cool giving bounce to my step

winter turns my green and gold to gray and silver
time slows for a long look inward:
one bird singing at dusk reminds me of spring

—2014

Saying Yes

A long history of saying *yes*
Or *maybe*, which quickly turned to *yes*
Or nothing, which is its own type of assent

Early training emphasized the importance of *No*
Safety, predictability lived in the land of *No*
One must save *yes* for special occasions

The turning toward *yes* as the majority
Position, choice, and rebellion
A way to learn why *No* had been
Taught, required, preferred

Yes led into new land
Discovery, sweet and sour
Abandoned to love and hate
But rich with life and truth

And now, living in the results of *No!* and *Yes!*
Searching for the balance
Knowing when there is a choice
Seeking perspective
To know the broad continuum
Between *yes* and *no*

—2014

123

In Transit

Cars and trucks and bikes and trikes
"The wheels on the bus go 'round and 'round"

Going walking moving transferring
Feet and wheels and boards and seats

So busy we are and eager to be on our way
To the next person appointment destination

Scheduled required impulsively moving
Hurried pushing running leaving

May I sit quietly now?
Finding peace in the smallest movements
Breathing blinking blood flowing
A gentle breeze on my face
Eyes closed to the rapid transit of humanity

—2014

Propinquity

My old heart, battered and broken again and again
Too tired, too laden with memories to try again

A life now with peace in my quiet home
My living companions, only three happy cats

Joy found in time with friends and family
Freedom to make music and art and literature

Then, one night, a dream, unbidden
Bright and clear upon waking as crystal glass
Newly washed and dried

Alone and lost in the rain, a man and his two children
Come to my aid, inviting me into a warm dry church
Then I am seated there alone, but content
Music begins, warming my heart

He slides smiling into the seat beside me
Suddenly the familiar sensation upon me
Being half a happy couple again, knowing
It to be so right, so comfortable, and a sweet ache at
Having missed it so much

Upon awakening, still awash in the emotions
Struggling to logically explain
This outrage

—2014

Loss and Love in the Circles of Life

Places of memory:
A cemetery
A headstone engraved Tanner, and now, another name

Just ashes, but those of
My Dad, My Mom, My Brother
Flood of tears with those memories

All together now in a place that each loved
We came to remember them and how
What they loved now lives on in us
Histories that are passed on to the next

Making new memories while awash in the old
Sharing stories
That might not otherwise have been told
Had we not walked together there

A release inside as we hurt together at the graveside
A need for it, hard to understand but true,
Sun dappled graves and flowers
Some wilting some bursting with
Newly picked colors
In the hands of grandchildren

Love crossing over time and through lives
Beyond death and reason, We Share,
Hear, Dare to Cry,
Walk, Remember, and Live

A few short months and one of us is gone, too
Still shocked at how sudden death can come
Unimaginable that one of those sweet grandchildren is
Now too ashes in a beautiful cemetery
And ashes nourishing a new tree
In the garden by her church

How one noisy and violent instant
Can change everything
Cause again the flood of tears and memories
Remember and savor
Those with whom we still may walk and love

—2014

2015

To Anders, The New One

Beautiful child, but a few hours since born
Sweet tiny grimace on a face perfectly formed
Eyes not so eager to open on this new world
And what do babies dream of
When they are newly born?

We caress and coo and wonder at tiny fingernails
Porcelain perfect ears, delicate lips and feet so small
Examining nose and cheeks
Compelled to compare these to his parents
Faces now awestruck, full with love and exhaustion.

And, I, a first-time grandparent, revel in this present
But also in my own memories,
Holding my first born brand new,
As I smile with her joy in the same.

He cries, and I rock him close, murmuring
It's so hard to be new, but being with one so new,
Our humanity expanded: new love and wonder
Gratitude for our existence and this holy mystery.

—2015

Nightmare

A dream woke me
Terror and sweat

A long tunnel tormenting me
Too much light too far

Crawling, walking, sliding to
Some goal implicit, assured
Certain, then a door

Locked, gray metal, antique knob
Of faceted crystal
Patina on the scratched copper

Immovable, unturnable,
Locked fast inscribed with reflections
Of my face full with terror
Distorted on a thousand tiny surfaces

Thankful for wakefulness
Breathing in my quiet house
My cat jumps to the forbidden mantel
I admire him

—2015

Downtown Haiku

Concrete overcast
Bright flashing yellow stoplight
Jackhammer please stop

—2015

Shadow Haiku

following my steps
disappearing with late dusk
sun awakens her

—2015

Longing for Lipstick

A sheltered loved little girl
Presbyterian proper family
But excited by Easter hats
And new red shoes

Less than happy about my clothes:
All hand-me-downs
Two older sisters assured that
I longed to have a dress just mine

I dreamed of a day
With high heels and garter belts
And bright red lipstick
And a hairdo sprayed into place

Then I would be a girl no longer
Meanwhile my mother's lipstick
Beckoned as she patiently
Taught her piano students downstairs

A fantasy come to life in her bedroom
Quickly ended in the bathroom
With soap and wash cloth
And I thought she never knew

—2015

On The Bus

Cello-toting teenager in her mini skirt on the city bus
(More like a very small-town bus)
A few coins are a gift of independence
Though, a short ride to the college campus,
Downtown, to school, to home

Sweet freedom for my limited travels
Loved the bike, but this feels grownup

Short years later busses take me to
New places, unknown, seen only on the map
Until I step down to the sidewalk

South American busses with chickens:
Legs tied together, curious children in rags
Iguanas with mouths sewn shut
Thieves preparing to steal my backpack
Learning to journey forward with less

Much later moving to a city where
My beloved busses do not travel
Widely or often enough
Car ownership, with repairs and licenses
Insurance and payments propel me through life

This new freedom of my own personal ride
Cross country trips, commutes with my own music

Temperature control and the occasional cry
Exhilaration in spontaneity has made it
Years now since I have set foot on a bus

Looking ahead to failing eyes and ears,
Slower reflexes, costs and dangers
Wondering if my final years of tromping
Riding, gliding about this earth will find me
Happy again to ride the bus

—2015

Eternity

You wonder about when you are gone
Dead that is, your living breathing hurting
Singing loving walking sleeping body
No longer alive
Your spirit gone from the physical frame

But how often you feel the presence of those
Gone now, but still walking with you
Breathing a smile into the nape of your neck
Glimpsed from behind, their words
Written in letters, books, programs and more
Remembered hurrying down an unlikely street

You look at photos and videos and listen to music
Read words and touch old fabrics
And you can almost taste and smell the essence
Of the departed soul
Of one who has left this realm

And then you think about the words and music
And photos and fabrics and smiles and touches
You will leave in your wake when it is your time
To depart, what tangible and intangible signs will
Awaken memories of you and how will that feel

You consider how documented your life has been
How so very increasingly often there are cameras
Recorders and video and omnipresent phones
At every occasion where you may be
Your words scattered all about
Letters, cards, books, cyberspace

You are in so many photo books
And videos of people who never knew your name
But valued your presence
And the music you brought that special day
As you played for their parties
Movies, weddings, recordings, lives

Then you wonder if this will be
Some kind of connection
To the living when you are no longer living
But your image, your sounds, your words
Are still in the world without you

—2015

Daisies

He loves me
He loves me not
One petal, then the next, and next

Where did I find all those daisies
And what did I learn from the dismemberment
Of their sweet faces

Sitting in the grass
With my girlfriend wondering
Which of us would be the one to be loved

We were loved, and then not
And then loved again, and then petals
Once again dropped forgotten to the ground

We got together last summer
No daisies, but many memories to share
To have been loved, and then not, again and again

—2015

Museum

That damn still life
Wilted chrysanthemums mocking me
Peeking out from some tacky gold frame

His musty house like a museum
Slippery memories echoing
A blurred photograph of wasted years

Behind the locked door of my denial
A shiny parquet floor beckons my bare feet
To slide on the wetness of melted ice
Coaxing hope for a fresh bed of yellow petals

—2015

Chance Meet

Quiet of a snowy morn
Captured snowflake moment

Tickling the tip of my tongue
The fleeting quietude, soul's balm

Don't run and stumble for it
Only stillness allows you to catch it

Quiet gratitude gazing upwards
Peace in presence with our world
Hello

—2015

Fly Free

Our fears fed by moving images
Fed to us on screens large and small
Vulnerable as a sleeping child
Or a soul struggling to take flight
Manipulations leave us numb to wonder
The child looks up and sees
Somehow denying fear
And embracing love

—2015

Picnic on the Fault Line

Smile at the arrival of your friend
Unannounced
And the music even finer than expected

Surprise gift ending the picnic
And gratitude for another day
Lived with fewer expectations

Happy sacrifice leads beyond hugs to joy
The pink and gold intimacy
Of a sunset over the roaring sea

One tiny flower blooms in the snow
Presage of a long anticipated reunion
With spring

An injury, betrayal, now long gone, fading scars
In retrospect, feeling like balance, or
Ballast in this push and pull of life

—2015

Christmas Dreams

Feeling like an old child this December
Sparkly lights and familiar music
A miracle story of birth and hope

Memories come in a flood of joy and sorrow
Bright young eyes smiling at the tree
Sad phone calls bringing tears and panic

Laughter and cookies, songs and snuggles
Stories of love and beginnings
Disappointments and death
Hugs of reassurance for those at the table

Along that winding road of seasons and scars
Each year keeps ending with this month
Meaning so much, and too little

I choose hope for those of us here
I seek faith for the journey ahead
I want love for each step and every encounter

A star, bright with promise
Shines through the moving clouds
And the dreams of Christmas move among us.

—2015

2016

Afternoon Spent With My Mother's Poetry

Three decades of poems
First second third drafts
Far more personal than any diary
Despair, joy, struggles, love,
Uncertainty, anger

Written in meter, or free, as haiku
And as assignments
Revelations of an era where change and family
Were often painful, frustrating, and sad

I found my name, my instrument
My life, among the many words:
A source of the pain in some
And in others, happy reminiscence
Family I never knew became
Fleshed out in her poems

Her own mother and grandmother
Holding her and comforting her
Her father taking the family camping
On his new land: discomfort and fear
Peaking out from brave faces

Tucked in a proud notebook
Of poems which had been published,
A musical crossword puzzle
Accepted for a magazine:
Those ten dollars in the return mail
A sweet source of pride

So much attention to the beauty of nature
A steadfastness at the surety of faith
A longing for authenticity
And a loving wonder of small things:
I thank her for these

A piano teacher for many years
She wrote of a student: he loved his lessons
And she so happy to open a world
Of music to him in his young life
A goddess, she called music

Her life so very present
In the scribbled corrections
Multiple copies with small changes
Me all these years later
Trying to find the final draft
To be true to her vision
As I arrange these precious sheets
Into a book she only dreamed of

—2016

Mirror

A face, my own, eyes still bright
Gray hairs aplenty, but I really don't mind
Too often I reject a photo for too old, too fat
A wrinkle, a bulge, a life time exposed

Is it lucky to have so many of my scars out of sight?
Could my vanity, still hanging on by a thread
Survive them out in the open each day?
But age can do that, as dreams of looking good
And sexy and healthy and athletic and attractive
Or maybe even beautiful and appealing,
All become unimportant, no longer sought after

I love it more now when people love my energy
My smile my feistiness my music my humor
My art my writing my love and compassion
Are these reflected in the mirror?
You need to be here with me
We need to be doing, talking, laughing, being
Together

And is it inevitable that it takes so long to learn this?
That the priorities of youth and culture and its stories
Expectations and the desire to please others
Can devour so many hours and so much
Of our love and precious energy that we do not see
To this beyond. A richness in these final years
Too precious to squander on the mirror.

—2016

Truth

To my self, can I ever be untrue?
We may lie, we do lie, but do we always know it?
Regretting, reveling, chuckling, or sweating:
pathological, compulsive, fantabulating,
unintentional, good intentioned, or just
trying to make the best of a bad situation?

A little encouragement,
something left unsaid out of kindness,
because total honesty is often brutal.

Do you want it? Do I?
From myself?

Glance in the mirror sideways,
listen to an account of your actions,
by someone who does not know you:
a look in another's eyes that you
were not meant to see.

Thinking, that honestly,
you can't actually do that.
Is a compromise a good idea?
Is truth the mark,
and just one's aim that is in question?

Is truthiness a word?
Can imagination become a lie?
Go ahead, try to be completely honest for one day.

—2016

Old Style

A font, a shoe, a ringing bell
My smile, my greeting, how do you do?

Why type, why walk, a sorry pun
Some days I wish my days were done...

Of course that is not true, my dear
I write now trying to meter some here.

Or perchance to rhyme a bit with wit
And should I finish, or maybe just quit?

What means Ms. Cameron to artist date
When with oneself it might be merely a debate?

To aspire to poetry is old school for sure
But now I can embrace this, fool or cure.

And whence the setting sun upon my brow
Tis a sweet and honeyed feeling
Yes, I do know how.

—2016

Prayer in the Cloister

Spindly trees, broad trees
tiny pink flowers alongside tall purple ones

An uneven number of women
bound only by their heart's desire
to grow, closer to the presence of the Eternal

To learn, to serve, to be grateful
more fully each day in our noisy world
What can separate us from our God?
Who is always here, and full in each moment
Unceasing among us

Only our distracted skittering minds
our broken hearts full of fear and doubt
too busy days full with striving for empty goals

Have Mercy, Eternal Father, help us
to have the strength to walk with you
every moment, and with each thought,
with every breeze we feel, melody we hear,
word we speak, and sweet taste that
graces our hungry mouths.
Let us smell the trees and the sea
with knowledge that these are your gifts to us.

Open our eyes dear Lord,
that we may see the need in the world,
the beauty all around us, and a lesson
in every moment.

—2016

Evolving Limitations

I could or should I
Yes, I once did, but not now?

Often the long day was filled
with nine hours of playing
but now six seems almost too much
or too tiring, or is this wisdom
learning to listen better to my body and soul

But how many are enough, or too many
or not enough?
Is there a limit for wishes wished,
or just for those fulfilled?
How many are now left?

Six hundred fifty miles driven in a day
cut down to three hundred fifty as optimum
a number that keeps moving.
Or hours on an airplane, listening to my legs
and my seat cry out for mercy.

If I don't have to any more, how many days
a week shall I present myself to bow for dollars?
Is there a life better to be lived
with purpose and pleasure and service
without commerce's distractions?

Limitations no longer as a negative
can they open a door, point to a path
show a new way
one that had been forgotten, lost, or neglected?

New limits arriving unexpectedly:
now why does that hurt there just now?
I thought I could do that.
It used to be easy.
Scrap the day's plans, but ahh, for better?

Reading, painting, writing,
napping, daydreaming, making music
are on the table. So mourn not
but savor the changes
born out of limitations.

—2016

2017

Saint Mary Time

Candles flicker in the sunlight
backed by reaching trees and blue skies
eight women faithful more than their number
pray, search, laugh, share
growing stronger
watching leaves flutter to the ground

We ask why, where, who, what
of our loving and eternal God
in whom all answers exist

Promised that we are made in God's image
we struggle to believe that life's mystery
in all its wonder and awe, beauty and pain,
inhabits our hearts and brains
and all the tiniest parts of our beings

So we beseech our Creator for guidance,
for strength, for peace patience love
and all the many gifts we know
that we have already received
with the gifts of these, our lives

Life as the greatest gift of grace:
we strive to be worthy, humble
to fulfill the promise of this gift
in each moment we walk this earth

—2017

December Muse

Prayers for the hurting
doubts and fears come bubbling up
amid the tinsel and fun
eager faces looking for joy
singing again as if for the first time

Traffic, rain, gray days
illuminated by twinkly lights
splashes of red, green, and gold
unexpected kindness touched by
the warmth of another soul

A seesaw, a boomerang
a tilt-a-whirl of a day
our human condition defined
the faithful still looking, hoping
peace seekers trying to live
by the light of a child

Beyond the fog and despair
see the glow, breathe deeply
a solstice preparation
for love and hope, grace
which is this gift of life

—2017

2018

Your Gentle

Your gentle rain a reminder
life as a gift that flows above and below
us in the middle

Your insistent downpour a call
to immediacy to look
be here now

Your softly falling snow a sigh
wet flakes full with memories
laughter and tears

Your bright sun an illumination
shining through puffy clouds
and the deep blue of eternity

A promise

—2018

Because of the Moon

I still breathe
Colors beguile me
Transcendence (in)forms intent

Words in shades
The aroma of life
laughter unleashed
push this body in its dance

Whirling, stumbling with
the beloved others, a shuffle
a dash, a slump

Do smile, touch, ask
Do not regret
or walk backwards

Your time is now
is all you know

—2018

The Author

Julia Tanner was born in Tulsa, Oklahoma, in 1949 and presently lives in Nashville, Tennessee. A cellist by profession, she served as assistant principal cellist for the Nashville Symphony from 1978 to 2015. She also played with the New Orleans Philharmonic, the National Canadian Opera Orchestra, the American Symphony, and the New York City Ballet Orchestra.

During her years in Nashville, she has also played on many recordings as a member of the Nashville String Machine and continues to work as a studio musician. She can be heard on the recordings of Garth Brooks, Amy Grant, Carrie Underwood, Martina McBride, Tim McGraw, Willie Nelson, Matchbox 20, Allison Krauss, and more. Several of her recordings with the Nashville Symphony won Grammy Awards. You can hear her solo playing on her self-produced CD, *Cello Prayers.* (Available on CD Baby and iTunes.)

A graduate of the Oberlin Conservatory of Music, she grew up nearby in Wooster, Ohio. There her father was head of the department of religion at the College of Wooster, while her mother was a piano teacher who also had a love for writing. Both of her parents encouraged her love for music, art, and the written word. For this, she feels very fortunate.